Phoenix, Arizona, home

1957 Rogers Majestic B+W TV

New Jersey house "bad tree of evil"

The TWILIGHT ZONE

Leah's Army surplus jeep late 1950s

STARRING STEVEN SPIELBERG

The Making of a Young Filmmaker

By **Gene Barretta** • Illustrated by **Craig Orback**

Christy Ottaviano Books

Little, Brown and Company

New York Boston

Meet a T. rex in *Jurassic Park*!
Communicate with peaceful aliens in *E.T.
the Extra-Terrestrial*! Hunt a killer shark in
Jaws! And search for lost treasures with
Indiana Jones in *Raiders of the Lost Ark*!

Steven Spielberg, one of the world's most influential filmmakers, tells stories about our world and beyond.

Yet, in many ways, he has also been telling us his own story.

In a town, in a theater, in an instant . . . one boy began a spectacular adventure. It all started with a catastrophic train wreck. Young Steven was there, eyes locked on the big screen as *The Greatest Show on Earth* lit up the movie theater.

"*I think my fate was probably sealed that day in 1952*," recalled Steven, reflecting on a lifetime of movie magic.

Ready? And . . .
ACTION!
Haddon Township, New Jersey, 1956. The Spielberg home was filled with entertainment. Dad told stories of adventure. Some were made up and some came from his days serving in World War II. Mom and Uncle Fievel filled the air with music. Great Uncle Boris kicked up his heels like he did back in the days of Yiddish theater and vaudeville. Steven joined in on clarinet! Mom taught the children to remain young at heart, like Peter Pan. *"We never grew up at home, because she never grew up."*

Dad exposed them to the wonders of science and technology through his work as an electrical engineer. Together, they nurtured Steven's creativity and intense curiosity for everything around him.

COMEDY! THRILLS! ADVENTURE!

Steven drew funny doodles in the corners of his books and watched them come to life when he flipped the pages. He was a natural storyteller.

One stormy day, Steven knocked down everything in the backyard and blamed it on an imaginary tornado.

Dinosaurs filled Steven's mind after he learned that his
town was once a prehistoric ocean. The first nearly complete
dinosaur skeleton was discovered in his neighborhood park over
one hundred years earlier. It was exciting to bring the dinosaurs
back to life when he eventually made the movie *Jurassic Park*.

Steven loved playing pranks—especially on his three sisters. He told them stories about a twenty-foot-tall bogeyman who peered into windows. He dressed up as monsters and lured them into homemade haunted houses.

Oddly enough, his pranks were a creative way to deal with his own fears. No one was more scared and anxious than Steven.

Sometimes his strong imagination backfired. Tree shadows on the bedroom wall became giant claws. He thought demons were calling to him from the TV static, when in fact it was just faded voices creeping through from another channel.

He never forgot those spine-tingling experiences and later put them both in a horror film he produced titled *Poltergeist*.

When the family moved to Phoenix, Arizona, Steven's anxiety peaked.

Dad's job changed several times. So did their address. So did Steven's friends. Wherever he lived, he felt like an outsider, like an alien from another planet.

It didn't help that some neighbors were not neighborly toward Jewish families. The Spielberg family was singled out with antisemitic slurs and threats. It became so stressful that Steven began to deny his Jewish heritage. *"All I wanted to do was fit in."*

Steven stood out at school. Kids made fun of his small, skinny frame and awkward features. They called him Spielbug, and it hurt. His grades took a dive, and bullies circled him like hungry sharks. School became more about survival and less about learning.

Those struggles haunted Steven and influenced his early films. Bullies showed up in all shapes and sizes.

Then, just as his world was turning upside down, "*I discovered something I could do, and people would be interested in it and me. . . . I would sit and watch the home movies and criticize the shaky camera movements and bad exposures until my father finally got fed up and told me to take over.*"

Home movies grew into works of art. Steven made them more entertaining by imitating shots he saw on TV shows. Family and friends became his actors. *"Staging real life was so much more fun than just recording it."*

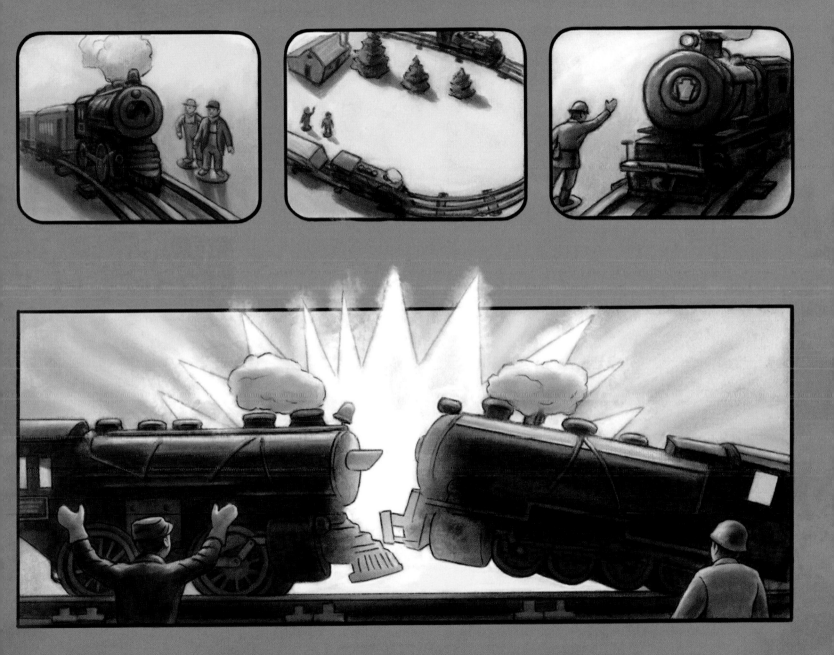

It wasn't long before he wrote his own stories. He even used model trains to re-create a big train wreck like the one he'd seen years earlier in *The Greatest Show on Earth.*

LIGHTS! CAMERA! POPCORN!

As a member of Boy Scout Troop 294, Steven created a short film that earned him both a merit badge and praise. The brotherhood he felt in the scouts motivated him to make more. *"It sort of brought out things I did well and forgave me for things I didn't."*

Home was transformed into a studio and a theater, where he showed movies to earn money for film and props. As neighbors watched the screen, Steven watched the neighbors. Why did they laugh? When did they scream? What made the characters interesting?

His audiences did not see the drama brewing off-screen. Mom and Dad were arguing more and more. Home was nothing like the "happy" American families he watched on television.

The stress at home caused Steven to let off steam the only way he knew: creative mischief. Like that day in science class when he saved several frogs from becoming science experiments.

In *E.T. the Extra-Terrestrial*, Elliott relives some of Steven's early experiences.

Steven tried to stay home from school as much as possible. Sometimes, he would fake having a fever by warming a thermometer under a light bulb. Elliott uses the same scheme on his mom in *E.T.*

Mom knew all his tricks but still loved keeping Steven home to play. It was not unusual to see them riding in her big Jeep, exploring the town during school hours.

His unofficial film school was the local Kiva movie theater. Steven and his friends studied Hollywood dramas, classic comedies, and adventure films with heroes who would later inspire the creation of Indiana Jones in *Raiders of the Lost Ark*.

The Indiana Jones films became an entire series of adventures.

Over time, Steven
learned how film directors
used powerful images to tell a story.
He studied how they moved their cameras
and how they edited shots together to make exciting
action scenes. There was nothing more fun than the
world he saw through his camera lens. Steven created
films from scratch and controlled every moment.

Dad's personal war stories inspired two of Steven's early films, *Fighter Squad* and *Escape to Nowhere*. Dad also pulled a few strings to get his son some authentic locations and vintage fighter planes for the action scenes.

To create the perfect illusion of a World War II airplane battle, Steven directed close-up shots of his friends sitting in old plane cockpits and combined that film with authentic footage of World War II airplanes. *"We didn't have any special effects expertise. . . . It was just 'how do you make this come to life?'"*

Battles on the ground were just as creative. No real explosions needed!
The actors launched dirt into the air by stepping on tiny seesaws.

Mom and Dad loved their son's passion and dedication. Despite their
differences, they pitched in however they could.

Due to his special interest in World War II,
Steven revisited the subject several times,
including in the epic film *Saving Private Ryan*.

Word spread about the young filmmaker. It wasn't long before local reporters showed up to interview him about *Escape to Nowhere*, which later won first prize in a statewide amateur film contest.

Steven came to life when making movies. He surprised everyone by directing his cast and crew with the skill and confidence of a Hollywood professional.

They were even more surprised when he gave the role of squadron leader to a tough school kid who taunted him for being Jewish. The boy's face was perfect for the part, and that's what mattered most to Steven. *"I was able to bring him over to a place where I felt safer. . . . I didn't use words. I used a camera. . . . I had learned that film was power."* That day, the bully saw another side of Steven.

Steven tackled antisemitism on a larger scale when he made *Schindler's List*, about a Nazi who saved the lives of 1,200 Jewish people during the Holocaust.

Playing sports and getting good grades did not come easy. Yet Steven was smart and creative, just like the kids in Drama Club. There, he could work with actors, paint scenery, operate the lights, learn makeup, even play clarinet with the orchestra. It was exciting to finally fit in somewhere. Friends affectionately called him the Big Spiel!

While still in high school, he began working on a new film. Steven had the determination and confidence to make something bigger: a feature-length film. Something he could show to the big movie studios.

Inspiration for Steven's new film came many years before, deep in the desert, when Dad gave him a front-row seat to a spectacular meteor shower. The bright slivers of light falling across the vast darkness of space made his earthly problems seem small. He didn't feel anxious. He looked up at the sky and saw all sorts of wonders.

The films *Close Encounters of the Third Kind* and *E.T. the Extra-Terrestrial* are very personal to Steven, as they recall the age when he became fascinated with space and alien visitors. Also, like the parents in both films, his parents were headed for divorce.

Take that night in the desert, add lots of imagination, mix in clever homemade special effects, spotlight mysterious alien visitors, and you've got *Firelight*, his first feature-length film. It was a huge accomplishment and deserved a huge neighborhood premiere.

FEEL THE SPIEL!

March 24, 1964. The Phoenix Little Theatre.

It was a night Steven had been dreaming about. Hundreds of people showed up to watch *Firelight*. Local TV stations covered the premiere. His parents rented a searchlight and limousine so Steven and his cast could drive up in style.

The audience loved it. Steven even made a small profit. Hard work paid off. For the budding director, it was the first of many highly anticipated premieres to come.

That night, as Steven's head hit the pillow, he truly was the Big Spiel. Don't you just love happy endings?

STARRING STEVEN SPIELBERG:
THE SEQUEL

Believe it or not, the day after the premiere, the Spielbergs moved to California. Another new job for Dad. For Steven, a new state meant new problems. Bullying got worse. He applied to film schools and was rejected by all of them. If that wasn't enough, Mom and Dad divorced. Steven was crushed.

CALIFORNIA

UNIVERSAL PICTURES
COMPANY INC.

Amblin'

A positive plot twist: They lived closer to the movie studios.

Life unfolded like a Hollywood movie. Act One: Steven got a summer apprenticeship at Universal Studios. Act Two: Steven made a short film called *Amblin'* and impressed the vice president of Production. Act Three: At age twenty-one, Steven became the youngest director to receive a contract at a major studio. It was time for him to start making the movies we all know and love.

"I visited every set I could, got to know people, observed techniques, and just generally absorbed the atmosphere."

Steven became a producer, cofounded a movie company, worked with celebrated actors, won major awards, and influenced a new generation of filmmakers.

Over the years, his personal life has been filled with its own rewards. His parents reunited after being apart for almost fifty years. Steven married and had a son. While that marriage ended, he later married actress Kate Capshaw. It was her encouragement, support, and personal religious journey that inspired Steven to re-embrace Judaism.

Together they have seven children.

Steven sums it up best: *"Hardly a single one of my films isn't based on something that happened in my childhood."*

AND THAT'S A WRAP!

FUN FACTS

1. Steven was born on December 18, 1946, in Cincinnati, Ohio.

2. In German, the word "Spielberg" translates to "Play Mountain." Steven's boyhood production company was called Play Mountain.

3. Steven has struggled with dyslexia his entire life but was not diagnosed until he was in his sixties.

4. In addition to being in Drama Club, Steven played clarinet for several years in the Ingleside Thunderbird Band. They played for school and sporting events, and special concerts.

5. In high school, Steven auditioned for a part in *Twelve Angry Jurors*, based on the play *Twelve Angry Men*. He was not cast, but he joined the crew and helped with lighting.

6. As a teen, Steven saw the classic film *Lawrence of Arabia*. He gave up his dream to become a film director because he thought he could never make a film that good. After watching it a few more times, he realized that making films was the only thing he wanted to do. It remains his favorite film, and he watches it at least once a year.

7. When he earned money from his neighborhood screenings, he always made sure to donate some to charity.

8. One way his parents helped out on his early films was to drive vehicles in scenes. After all, no one else was old enough.

9. Steven likes the fact that he still has anxiety when he arrives on the set. He says, "*I need to feel that in this moment, I'm really not sure what I'm doing. And when that verges on panic, I get great ideas.*"

10. The film *Saving Private Ryan* was a gift to his dad. *Schindler's List* was a gift to his mom.

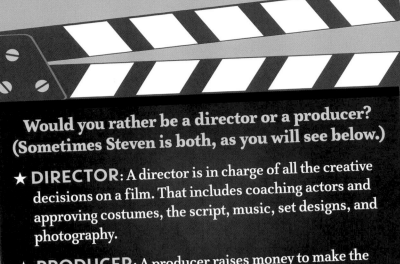

Would you rather be a director or a producer?
(Sometimes Steven is both, as you will see below.)

★ **DIRECTOR**: A director is in charge of all the creative decisions on a film. That includes coaching actors and approving costumes, the script, music, set designs, and photography.

★ **PRODUCER**: A producer raises money to make the film. Producers also help hire the director, the cast, and much of the crew. They oversee all phases of the production and schedule.

Recommended for Younger Viewers
(G and PG ratings)

1. *Close Encounters of the Third Kind* (Director, Writer)
2. *Indiana Jones and the Raiders of the Lost Ark* (Director)
3. *E.T. the Extra-Terrestrial* (Director, Producer)
4. *Hook* (Director)
5. *Empire of the Sun* (Director, Producer)
6. *The Adventures of Tintin* (Director, Producer)
7. *The BFG* (Director, Producer)
8. *Gremlins* (Executive Producer)
9. *The Goonies* (Executive Producer)
10. **Back to the Future series** (Executive Producer)
11. *An American Tail* (Executive Producer)
12. *Who Framed Roger Rabbit* (Executive Producer)

Recommended for Teens and Older Viewers (PG, PG13, and R ratings)

1. *Jaws* (Director)
2. *Schindler's List* (Director, Producer)
3. *Saving Private Ryan* (Director, Producer)
4. *Poltergeist* (Producer)
5. *Jurassic Park* (Director)
6. *Indiana Jones and the Temple of Doom* (Director, Producer)
7. *Men in Black* (Executive Producer)
8. *Ready Player One* (Director, Producer)

Please consult an adult for film ratings to confirm that content is age appropriate.

Quote Sources

5. *"I think my fate was probably sealed that day in 1952."*: Said during his acceptance speech for the Cecil B. DeMille Award at the 2009 Golden Globes. https://www.youtube.com/watch?v=NV8k4tNCB6k

6. *"We never grew up at home, because she never grew up."*: Joseph McBride, *Steven Spielberg: A Biography* (Jackson: University Press of Mississippi; Second Edition, 2011). Page 32.

13. *"All I wanted to do was fit in."*: Said in an interview in the documentary *Spielberg*, directed by Susan Lacy (HBO Documentary Films, 2017).

16. *"I discovered something I could do, and people would be interested in it and me."*: McBride, *Steven Spielberg: A Biography*. Page 62.

17. *"Staging real life was so much more fun than just recording it."*: Molly Haskell, *Steven Spielberg: A Life in Films.* (New Haven: Yale University Press; Illustrated Edition, 2017). Page 53.

18. *"It sort of brought out things I did well and forgave me for things I didn't."*: McBride, *Steven Spielberg: A Biography*. Page 67.

24. *"We didn't have any special effects expertise."*: Steven Jay Rubin, *Combat Films: American Realism 1945–2010.* McFarland & Co. Page 226.

27. *"I was able to bring him over to a place where I felt safer."*: McBride, *Steven Spielberg: A Biography*. Page 91.

35. *"I visited every set I could, got to know people, observed techniques."*: McBride, *Steven Spielberg: A Biography*. Page 99.

37. *"Hardly a single one of my films isn't based on something that happened in my childhood."*: Richard Schickel, *Steven Spielberg: A Retrospective.* (New York: Sterling, 2012). Page 1.

38. *"I need to feel that in this moment, I'm really not sure what I'm doing."*: Said in an interview in the documentary *Spielberg*.

For Stuart Reeves, John Desiderio, and Yen Lucas.
My personal E.T.s when the galaxy feels topsy-turvy. —GB

For all children and parents like Steven
who have known the heartbreak of divorce. —CO

ABOUT THIS BOOK

The illustrator used Cretacolor Monolith 6B pencils on Canson paper, and painted and inked the art in Procreate and Photoshop. This book was edited by Christy Ottaviano and designed by Véronique Lefèvre Sweet. The production was supervised by Nyamekye Waliyaya, and the production editor was Andy Ball. The text was set in Atma Serif TF Medium Roman, and the display type is Core Circus.

Arcadia
High
School
Library

Shed where he
filmed train crash
movie

Anne   Sue   Nancy   early
1960s

Anne
1966

Carport of Phoenix, Arizona,
home 1964